This book is to be returned on or before
the last date stamped below.

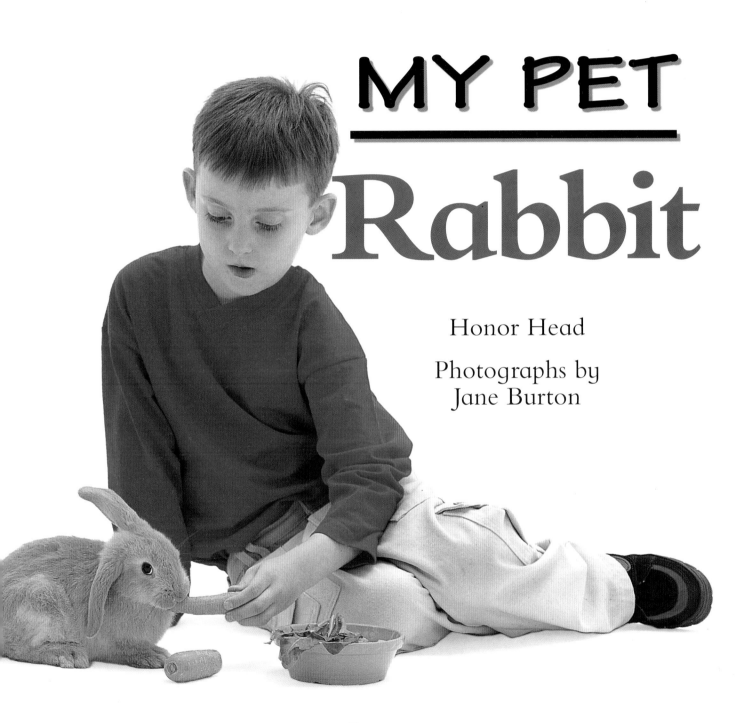

MY PET

Rabbit

Honor Head

Photographs by
Jane Burton

Belitha Press

First published in the UK in 2000 by
Belitha Press Limited, London House,
Great Eastern Wharf, Parkgate Road,
London SW11 4NQ

ISBN 1 84138 085 7

British Library Cataloguing in Publication
Data for this book is available from the
British Library.

Editor: Claire Edwards
Designer: Rosamund Saunders
Illustrator: Pauline Bayne
Consultant: Frazer Swift

Printed in Singapore

10 9 8 7 6 5 4 3 2 1

PDSA (People's Dispensary for Sick Animals)
is Britain's largest charity which each year
provides free treatment for some 1.4 million
sick and injured animals of disadvantaged
owners.

A royalty of 2.5 per cent of the proceeds from
this book will be paid to the PDSA (People's
Dispensary for Sick Animals) on every copy
sold in the UK.

The products featured have been kindly
donated by Pets at Home.

Contents

My rabbit

ears

nose

fur

paws

claws

It's fun owning your own pet.

Rabbits look very sweet and are fun to have as pets, but they need to be looked after carefully.

A rabbit needs feeding every day. You will have to clean out its hutch and make sure that it is happy and healthy. Most of all, remember that your rabbit may be with you for many years.

Young children with pets should always be supervised by an adult. For further notes, please see page 32.

There are many different types of rabbits.

Some rabbits have long, fluffy fur. They look very soft, but they need to be groomed every day.

A big rabbit may be too heavy for you to pick up when it is full grown. They need lots of space and eat more than smaller rabbits.

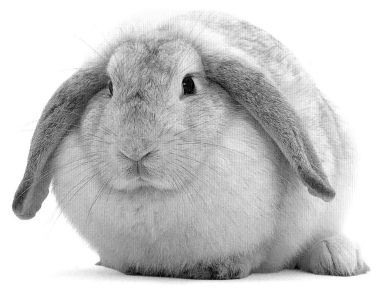

Lop-eared rabbits have long, droopy ears. You have to be careful to keep their ears clean.

Some rabbits are bred specially for their markings, such as spots, splodges and patches. Some have coloured ears, face and feet.

This rabbit is a dwarf rabbit. Small rabbits are easier to pick up and won't eat as much as big rabbits.

When baby rabbits are born they are helpless.

When a rabbit is pregnant she uses fur from her tummy to make a soft nest for her babies.

A mother rabbit does not look pregnant until about a week before the babies are born. Give her more food and drink, but do not touch her.

Rabbits usually have about five babies, but some rabbits may have as many as ten.

Newborn rabbits do not have any fur. They cannot see or hear. Do not look at them until they are at least three weeks old.

Rabbits grow very quickly.

Baby rabbits are called kittens. When they are very small do not pick them up or touch them.

When the kitten is three weeks old it has all its fur. Its eyes are wide open and it can run and jump about.

A kitten's fur shows at four days. Its eyes open at about one week.

Kittens find their way to their mother's milk by smell. Drinking their mother's milk is called suckling.

A kitten is old enough to leave its mother when it is about eight weeks old.

Your rabbit needs a cosy place to live.

Have a hutch ready for your new pet. The hutch should have two parts, one you can see into and one where the rabbit can sleep.

Your rabbit will also need a water bottle and a food bowl.

If the hutch is outside, make sure it is raised so that it doesn't get wet. Your rabbit must have shelter from the sun, rain and wind.

Cover the floor of the hutch with newspaper and sawdust or wood shavings. Put in lots of hay where the rabbit will sleep.

Put a large wire hutch (called a run) in the garden for your rabbit. Make sure the run is strong and can't be knocked over. Move it from time to time so that your rabbit has fresh grass to eat.

Your rabbit will like to be held.

Your rabbit may be scared of you at first.
Leave it in its hutch for a day before you
pick it up. Then stroke the rabbit gently
so that it grows used to you.

Talk quietly to your rabbit
so that it gets used to
the sound of your voice.
Always stroke a rabbit
in the direction its
fur grows.

Sit or kneel to pick up your rabbit. Place one hand under its chest, behind its front legs. Use your other hand to scoop up its bottom. Never squeeze your rabbit or pick it up by its ears.

If your rabbit struggles, put it down gently. Place its back legs on the floor first. Never drop your rabbit or you will hurt it.

You can train your rabbit.

If you let your rabbit run around indoors, train it to use a litter tray. Watch where it goes to the toilet and leave the litter tray there.

Empty the litter tray every day. Wash it with warm water and disinfectant once a week. Wear rubber gloves when cleaning your rabbit's tray.

If your rabbit does something it shouldn't, such as trying to kick you, say 'no'. Do not hit your rabbit. When it stops being naughty, give it something to eat.

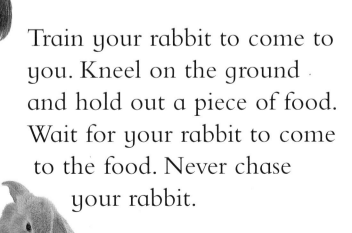

Train your rabbit to come to you. Kneel on the ground and hold out a piece of food. Wait for your rabbit to come to the food. Never chase your rabbit.

Your rabbit likes to eat at regular times.

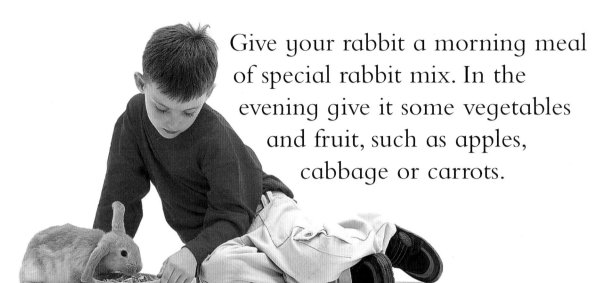

Give your rabbit a morning meal of special rabbit mix. In the evening give it some vegetables and fruit, such as apples, cabbage or carrots.

Put the food in a heavy bowl or your rabbit may knock it over. Always wash fresh food and cut it into small chunks. Take away any stale food.

Make sure your rabbit has enough water. Buy a special water bottle and make sure it is filled with fresh water all the time.

Your rabbit should have lots of hay to munch during the day.

Rabbits also enjoy parsnips and celery. If you can, pick some clover or dandelion leaves for your pet.

Keep your rabbit's hutch clean.

Clear away your rabbit's droppings and any wet wood shavings every day.

Clean the hutch once a week – more when the weather is hot. Throw away old bedding and sweep out the hutch. Put in clean bedding and wood shavings.

Every two weeks give the hutch a real clean out. Put your rabbit in a safe place. Rinse the hutch with soapy water and spray it with a special disinfectant from a pet shop.

Wash out your rabbit's water bottle at least once a week. Use a bottle brush, which you can buy from a pet shop.

Your rabbit will want to play.

Your rabbit will need plenty of exercise. It will enjoy exploring in the garden or indoors.

If your rabbit is running about indoors, keep the doors and windows shut. Always stay in the room with your rabbit when it is exploring.

Rabbits are very curious. Leave out boxes or baskets for your pet to explore.

Don't let your rabbit chew any wires or cables. Make sure sharp objects, such as scissors or pins, are out of reach.

Make sure your rabbit is healthy.

Most rabbits keep their
own fur clean and healthy.
But they also like to
be brushed.

Use a soft brush and brush your
pet from its head down to its
tail. Gently stroke underneath
your rabbit's body to
remove any bedding
caught in its fur.

Your rabbit will need a mineral block to chew. This will help to keep your pet healthy.

Give your rabbit a log or a wooden block to gnaw on to stop its teeth growing too long.

Look at your rabbit carefully every day. If your rabbit has dull fur, runny eyes, nose or ears, or an upset tummy, take it to the vet as soon as possible.

Your rabbit will want a friend.

In the wild, rabbits live in groups so your rabbit will enjoy having a friend. Female rabbits from the same litter make a perfect pair.

Rabbits get on well with guinea pigs if they meet when they are both young. Make sure they have enough space in the hutch.

Do not put a
female rabbit with
a male that has not
been neutered. They
will have lots of
kittens and you will
not be able to look
after them.

Rabbits and cats or
dogs can get on
together if they meet
when they are both
very young. Usually
you should keep cats
and dogs away from
your rabbit.

Rabbits can live for eight years or more.

Rabbits can live for up to about
12 years. As your rabbit gets older
check that it is eating properly.
Let it sleep more if it wants to
and help it to keep its fur clean.

As rabbits grow older
their claws may grow
too long. A vet will
trim them for you.

Like people, rabbits grow old and eventually die. If your rabbit is very old or ill, it may be kinder to let the vet put it to sleep.

You may feel sad when your pet dies, but you will be able to look back and remember all the happy times you had together.

Words to remember

bedding Hay and straw for a rabbit to sleep in.

groom To brush and comb an animal. Animals groom themselves with their teeth and tongue.

hutch The name of the home where a pet rabbit lives.

kitten A baby rabbit.

litter tray A rabbit's toilet.

neutered When an animals has been neutered, it has been operated on so that it cannot have babies.

run A long hutch made of wire and wood, where a rabbit can play outside.

suckling When a baby rabbit drinks its mother's milk it is suckling.

vet An animal doctor.

Rabbits grow fast.

One week old.

Three weeks old.

Eight weeks old.

Index

Notes for parents

A rabbit will give you and your family a great deal of pleasure, but it is a big responsibility. If you decide to buy a rabbit for your child, you will need to ensure that the animal is healthy, happy and safe. You will also have to care for it if it is ill, and supervise your child with the animal until he or she is at least five years old. It will be your responsibility to make sure your child does not harm the rabbit and learns to handle it correctly.

Here are some other points to think about before you decide to own a rabbit:

- Some rabbits can be bad-tempered and can bite, kick and scratch. Choose your rabbit carefully. Dwarf rabbits are easier for young children to look after.

- A rabbit can live for 12 years and costs money to feed and neuter. As it gets older, you may have to pay vet's bills.

- When your rabbit is a year old you should take it to the vet. The vet can give it an injection against serious diseases.

- When you go on holiday, you will need to make sure someone can care for your rabbit.

- Unless you are breeding rabbits, both males and females should be neutered.

- It is better to keep two rabbits together. Two females from the same litter are ideal, but males and females from the same litter can be kept together if the male is neutered. Two males from the same litter can be kept together, but they must be neutered to prevent them from fighting.

- If you have other pets, will the rabbit get on with them?

- Rabbits fed on the latest complete diets should not be fed mineral supplements unless specifically advised by a vet.

This book is intended as an introduction only for young readers. If you have any queries about how to look after your pet rabbit, you can contact the PDSA (People's Dispensary for Sick Animals) at Whitechapel Way, Priorslee, Telford, Shropshire TF2 9PQ. Tel: 01952 290999.